OUR PLANET OUR FUTURE

HELPING THE PEOPLE

Written by
Azra Limbada

Cavendish Square

New York

Published in 2022 by Cavendish Square Publishing, LLC
29 East 21st Street
New York, NY 10010

Website: cavendishsq.com

This publication represents the opinions and views of the author based on his or her
personal experience, knowledge, and research. The information in this book serves as
a general guide only. The author and publisher have used their best efforts in preparing
this book and disclaim liability rising directly or indirectly from the use and application of
this book.

All websites were available and accurate when this book was sent to press.

Edited by: John Wood
Designed by: Drue Rintoul

Cataloging-in-Publication Data
Names: Limbada, Azra.
Title: Helping the people / Azra Limbada.
Description: New York : Cavendish Square, 2022. | Series: Our planet, our future |
Includes glossary and index.
Identifiers: ISBN 9781502663535 (pbk.) | ISBN 9781502663559 (library bound) |
ISBN 9781502663542 (6 pack) | ISBN 9781502663566 (ebook)
Subjects: LCSH: Environmental protection--Juvenile literature. | Environmental
responsibility--Juvenile literature. | Climatic changes--Juvenile literature.
Classification: LCC TD170.15 L563 2022 | DDC 363.7--dc23

Some of the images in this book illustrate individuals who are models. The depictions do
not imply actual situations or events.

CPSIA compliance information: Batch #CW22CSQ: For further information contact Cavendish Square Publishing LLC, New York, New York,
at 1-877-980-4450.

Printed in the United States of America

Find us on

PHOTO CREDITS

Images are courtesy of Shutterstock.com. With thanks to Getty Images, Thinkstock Photo and iStockphoto. Cover - "Aid workers treat Haitians" flickr photo by United States Marine Corps Official Page https://
flickr.com/photos/marine_corps/4312104592 shared as a United States Government Work (PD). Anton_Ivanov. 4&5 - Sergey Novikov, Wirestock Images. 6&7 - Thomas La Mela, Martina Strihova. 8&9 - John-Kelly,
Kodda. 10&11 - NadyGinzburg, LifetimeStock. 12&13 - eggeegg, spass, Peteri. 14&15 - Artur Synenko, Piyaset, LightField Studios. 16&17 - Syda Productions, CGN089. 18&19 - fivepointsix, Salvacampillo. 20&21 - Per
Grunditz, Anna Om. 22&23 - Blacknote, KAMONRAT, Lunatictm, Andrey Maximenko, Belish, Etaphop photo, New Africa, Nils Z, mihalec, Anton Starikov.

CONTENTS

Words that look like this can be found in the glossary on page 24.

EARTH

Our planet is called Earth. There are lots of different living things on Earth, from tiny bugs to giant elephants.

EARTH IS BEAUTIFUL.

WHAT CAN YOU SEE?

Can you see the green grass?
Can you see the long, winding river?

EARTH IS HOME TO ALL OF US!

HUMANS

We share Earth with lots of different animals and plants. There are lots of people on the planet, and the things we do make a big difference to the world.

THERE ARE AROUND 7.7 BILLION PEOPLE ON EARTH.

It is our job to keep our planet healthy and safe. We need to work together to protect the <u>environment</u> and all the animals who share our home.

ENERGY

Energy makes things move and work. We use energy to do things such as heat a home or drive a car. Energy powers our world!

ELECTRICITY IS A TYPE OF ENERGY. IT IS CARRIED TO DIFFERENT PLACES USING WIRES.

FOSSIL FUELS

Oil, coal, and gas are <u>fossil fuels</u>. Most of the energy in the world comes from burning fossil fuels. We burn fossil fuels to drive cars, fly planes, and use electricity.

THESE BUILDINGS ARE BURNING LOTS OF COAL TO MAKE ENERGY.

AIR POLLUTION

Burning fossil fuels gives off harmful <u>gases</u>, which drift into the <u>atmosphere</u>. The harmful gases cause <u>climate change</u>, which is very bad for our planet.

THE HARMFUL GASES ARE A TYPE OF AIR <u>POLLUTION</u>.

Climate change makes it very difficult for people, animals, and plants to live. It can cause more dangerous weather or make it too hot or cold to live in some places.

CLIMATE CHANGE HAS MADE ICE MELT AROUND THE NORTH POLE. ANIMALS NEED THE ICE TO LIVE.

WAYS TO HELP

There are lots of ways you can help! Using less electricity means that less fossil fuels will be burned.

SWITCH OFF LIGHTS WHEN YOU DON'T NEED THEM.

THE AMOUNT OF AIR POLLUTION YOU CAUSE BY USING FOSSIL FUELS IS CALLED YOUR CARBON FOOTPRINT.

You can help by walking to school instead of driving. If there are fewer cars driving around, it means there will be less air pollution.

RIDING YOUR BIKE IS A GREAT WAY TO HELP KEEP OUR PLANET HEALTHY!

TAKING THE BUS IS ALSO BETTER THAN DRIVING IN A CAR.

FOOD AND WATER

The air pollution that creates climate change also affects our food and water. Growing <u>crops</u> becomes more difficult if climate change causes too much or too little rainfall.

FLOODING AND <u>DROUGHTS</u> CAN ALSO DESTROY CROPS.

Wasting food also wastes the energy that was used to make it. Always be careful of how much food you throw away and don't buy more than you need!

EAT UP TO SAVE THE ENVIRONMENT!

GROW YOUR OWN FOOD!

The food you buy at the supermarket is often grown far away. A lot of fossil fuels are burned to move the food from place to place, until it gets to the supermarket shelves.

Growing your own food or buying from nearby farms helps the environment. You could help cut down on all the harmful gases that are made from burning fossil fuels.

GARDENING IS SO MUCH FUN!

CLIMATE REFUGEES

Some people are forced to <u>migrate</u> because changes in the environment make it hard for them to live in their own countries. These people are called climate refugees.

CLIMATE CHANGE IS CAUSING MORE FLOODS AROUND THE WORLD.

THERE ARE MORE AND MORE CLIMATE REFUGEES EVERY DAY.

Climate refugees might travel very far to look for a safe place to stay. Their homes might have been destroyed by floods or other types of <u>extreme</u> weather.

THIS IS A CAMP SET UP FOR PEOPLE WHO LOST THEIR HOMES TO EXTREME WEATHER.

GRETA THUNBERG

This is Greta Thunberg. She is an <u>activist</u> who is trying to stop climate change. Greta wants everyone to work together to help save our planet.

Greta also wants to plant lots of new trees. Trees help keep our planet healthy in many different ways. They take in the harmful gases and make good homes for many animals.

MAKE YOUR OWN ECO ROBOT

Here's everything you need to make your own eco robot friend.

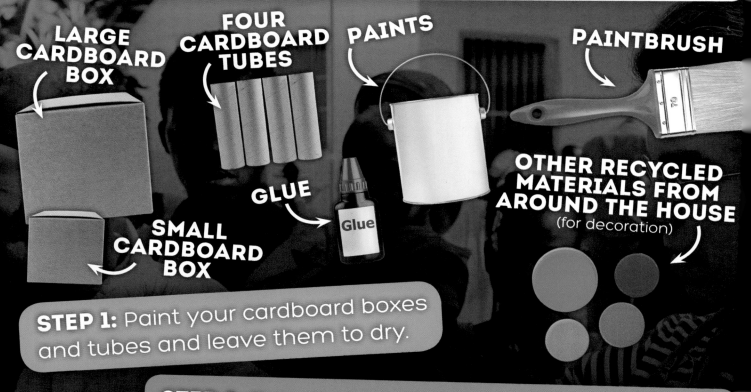

LARGE CARDBOARD BOX

FOUR CARDBOARD TUBES

PAINTS

PAINTBRUSH

GLUE

SMALL CARDBOARD BOX

OTHER RECYCLED MATERIALS FROM AROUND THE HOUSE (for decoration)

Glue

STEP 1: Paint your cardboard boxes and tubes and leave them to dry.

STEP 2: Take the smaller box. This will be the head. Glue it to the bigger box, which will be the body.

STEP 3: The cardboard tubes will be the legs and arms. Glue them to the body.

STEP 4: Decorate your robot with other recycled materials. For example, plastic bottle lids make good eyes or buttons!

23

GLOSSARY

activist	someone who tries to bring about a change by speaking out
atmosphere	the gases surrounding Earth
climate change	a change in the typical weather or temperature of a large area
crops	food and plants grown on a farm
droughts	long periods of time without rainfall, which leads to a lack of water
environment	the natural world
extreme	far beyond something usual
fossil fuels	fuels, such as coal, oil, and gas, which formed millions of years ago from the remains of animals and plants
gases	things that are like air, which spread out to fill any space available
migrate	to move from your home country to another
pollution	something added to our environment that is harmful to living things

INDEX